THE JOURNEY OF DREAMS

ATINDERPAL SINGH

This book is dedicated to every mother and love in the world, which
become the reason for living life,

Atinderpal Singh

Contents

Contents

Foreword

"Life can never be like a dream, but every dream has a life."

Atinderpal Singh, The Journey of Dreams (by the author).

If we feel that life and books both feel very close to each other. Our whole life changes based on thinking, age and experience. At every step of the way, there is something new to learn from life. Through my book, "The Journey of Dreams", which is a question in itself, I have tried to bring life closer as possible, like raindrops meet ever-burning sand. Life is full of questions, but the answers to many of your questions are hidden inside. My aim is to collect pearls with the thread of words and give courage to the sad, melancholy life through the garland of happiness so that the reader can feel the happiness of life through this book and dare to move towards his destination. The book includes common words as well as experiences and examples of some great personalities to help you understand every aspect of life in detail. Of course, these examples may be true or fictional but the real purpose of this book is to focus only on the consequences while dispelling the truth and fiction. Just as the meaning of life may differ according to different thinking, so it is natural for human beings to have different views on some of these examples. But with all these words, I try to give a reason to every human being who has knelt before life. Like a spark for a fire and a small hole becomes the main role for releasing trapped water. Although this book is incapable of fully describing human life in the court of readers, it is a must for every reader to find the reasons for living life in

this book. . So let's try to enjoy life happily again.
    Atinderpal Singh

Thanks Words

To write this book, the hard work of many people isinvolved. The examples, stories and events used in this book are based on social media, newspapers, magazines etc. Every effort has been made to publish the words used for the example with the name of the author, if the name of any author has been left to publish due to inappropriate information, for that please forgive me and the audience can share their thoughts about this book, for them every possible effort will be made to give respect to their information in the next edition. Thank you all for contributing to this book. To turn my dreams in reality and for making this book better Davinder Verma, Satbir Singh Parmar, Preet Simr, Gurpinder Singh Brar, Kuldeep Singh Kanth, Ramandeep Singh Brar, Mandeep Singh Brar, Ravinder Singh Brar, Navdeep Kumar, Sahil Sharma, Harpreet Romana and Harmanpreet Singh thank you to all friends. Why was it necessary to include the views of different personalities in the book? Through this book every aspect of life has been presented in better way, in which an attempt has been made to explain on the basis of positive thinking and experiences that life in itself is deep ocean. The amount of information will get about it, it would be little .

"Life can never be like a dream, but there is a life inevery dream."

Atinderpal Singh

Preface

According to this thought my single mindedness and outlook on life was probably not enough. My goal is to give you a strong and positive outlook through every possible effort. Therefore, it was felt necessary to record the views of various personalities in a suitable place in this book. In simple words, an attempt has been made to explain in very simple words. These different thoughts will work to bring a pause in your mind. Rather than read this book feel it. Read each part and inspect it according to your own thinking. A blank page is provided at the end of each section. An observation made on this page will bring you closer to your life and happiness. The ideasof different personalities, which are included in the appropriate place in each section, can play a very important role for you. A list of all those ideas has been published separately.

1 "Any new beginning means the end of somethingelse - Blair Wordoff

2. Be patient, everything seems difficult before itbecomes easy. -Sadi

3. "The man who asks questions becomes a fool for a minute, but the person who does not ask questions becomes a fool for the rest of his life" Confucius

4. "If you are born poor, there is nothing wrong with you but If you are poor at the time of death, then youare responsible for this mistake." Bill Gates

5. "If you want children to keep their feet on the ground, put some responsibility on their shoulders."Polin Phillips

6. In youth, work for learn, not to earn for learn, notto earn in youth "Robert Kiosk

7. Knowing a little about the setting sun does not detract from its thrill - Carl Sangan

8."All religious granths has read but peace to mind and brain that has met from reading Sikh's granth sahib never met from any other granth sahib". Pearl S. Bank

9. "Sikhs are also to blame for the message of Sikhism not reaching the world. No one else, Sikhism is not the property of Sikhs but it came into existence for the betterment of all humanity - Bertrand Russell

10" Eat good, read books, read yourself, develop the mind, do good and become good.

11.Last but not least, remember that your most important investment is inyourself "- Warren Buffett.

12. "Imagination always brings us in such a world that is not possible but without it we cannot go anywhere". Napoleon Hill

13. "The most dangerous is the direction in which the sun of the soul sets and its dead sunlight stings in the east of your body. Looting of labor is not the most dangerous, beating by police is not the most dangerous, betrayal - greed is not the most dangerous." Avtar Singh Pash

14" Passing life by doing mistakes is far more honourable than staying free." - George Bernard Shaw

15. "If you don't have time for the little things then you will not have time for the big things". Richard Bonson

16. "Thousands miles journey start with a single step."Laozi

17. "You can't plan for the future with the past." EdmundBurke

18. "There is no need to stress about the problem we can solve, on the contrary, there is no need to stress about the problem we can't solve." - Adolf Hitler

19. "Every bird finds shelter during the rain, but the eagle flies over the clouds to avoid the rain. "A. P. J. Abdul Kalam

20," Wake up and don't stop until the goal is achieved" - Swami Vivekananda Swami

21. ""Run if you can't fly, walk if you can't run, if you can't walk then crawl - But keep walking always." Martin Luther King, Junior

22." "Experience is the only source of knowledge" - Albert Einstein

23 "The key to success is confidence. The key to self-confidence is preparation "- Arthur Ash"

24. "I don't walk on the roads, when I walk the roads are built, caravans have been witnesses to this truth for centuries." Surjit Pater

25. "I don't believe in making the right decision, I make the decision and make it right" - Ratan Tata

26. "You have limited time, don't waste it living forsomeone else" - Steve Jobs

27. "Take a closer look at nature and you'll get to know everything better" Albert Einstein

28. "Accept the responsibilities of your life. Know that you can take yourself where you want to go. No one else willtake you - Les Brown.

29. "Winning or losing is part of the game, it shouldnot be taken to heart."- Milkha Singh

30. "For big wins, take big risks" - Bill Gates

31. "If you want to shine like the sun, first learn toburn like it." -A.P.J Abdul Kalam

32. "No one can go back and start, but they can start today and end a new," said Marie Robinson

33. "The greatest discovery of my generation is that man can change his life by changing his attitude - William

James

34. "Sometimes happiness become a cause of smiling. But sometimes our smile become the cause of ourhappiness ... -Tick Naat Haan

35. "you take the first step towards success only when you think about getting out of the current environment?" -Mark Kane

36 "Keep your face towards the sun, the shadows willfollow you" - Walt Whitman

CHAPTER ONE

The beginning of life with dreams

Life begins with birth. This journey continues passthrough different parts. In every part, one or the other dream must be seen. Dreams are often seen as a way of life. With hard work, dreams can come true. If your attitude is positive and you can dare to think differently from the world, then these dreams lead to happiness. But if we make no effort to fulfil the dreams, then the dreams that cause this happiness become mountains of sorrow for us. Everyone has different accidents in their life and everyone faces these accidents differently. The power of dreams is a means of proving our skills and inspiring us to work hard. Only your freedom of thought can bring happiness into your life. A comfortable life can be connected to your dream. But even if you feel suffocated in such an environment, it proves to be a slave to your thinking. Because sometimes we make a habit of living a life of luxury and force our thoughts and ideas to compromise. Your dreams can take you from one country to another. Where you feel alone in the majority of people of other religions and races. This feeling starts to weaken you from within. If you are in the right place, you do not have to compromise. Only raising your voice for your rights can save your dream from dying. The revolutionary element must always be burning in your thoughts. You may have to go through physical and mental hardships due to these revolutionary ideas but your free-thinking will fill you with strange peace and give you happiness. You should be happy to make the decision according to your own thinking. With the help of this strong thinking, you can overcome every adversity and move forward according to your thinking. "Sometimes the body has to be enslaved to keep the ideas free - Atinderpal Singh Any new beginning means the end of something else - Blair Werdoff Let's start the dream anew. In this beginning, we will do our best to make dreams come true by making positive thinking and hard work as our partner. Your different thinking will bring you in front of the same thinking that has been going on from generation to generation. The purpose of the crowd standing in front of you is to destroy your thoughts and dreams. So this path of free-thinking can lead you to happiness, but you must be prepared to face the difficulties of your path. Your right or wrong cannot guarantee your victory and the result will be blurred until you can make your thinking a movement and your thinking don not give birth to a caravan to face the crowd. Only revolutionary thought can make slave dreams free by becoming a movement. Never let dreams become slaves, recognize your strength. "Be patient, everything seems difficult before it becomes easy. Sadi" your whole focus should be on turning your dream's world into reality, the fear of difficulties will not stop you from taking action. There is very little difference between wisdom and foolishness, just need to understand this difference. If you have a clear commitment to your dreams, then the fear of the consequences will not be an obstacle for you. Your decision to start will be a testimony of wisdom. "Steps are not taken by looking at the results, if steps are taken then results are produced. But if you do not know the direction of your dreams, you have no attachment to your dreams, these dreams cannot find their goal, then it would be foolish to take steps without thinking. Learn to ask yourself questions, the answer to every question is hidden inside you. Instead of looking down on others, try to stand up for yourself. "A person who asks a question becomes a fool for a minute, but he who does not ask becomes a fool for the rest of his life". - - Confucius Life and the journey of dreams go hand in hand. They end their existence without each other. Because there can be no interest in life without dreams and life cannot be interesting without dreams. The journey of dreams can lead you to happiness only if you have a positive attitude towards life. Dare to put yourself in the court of questions. To make your sad and helpless life as colourful as dreams try to understand it in a better way. Let your thinking flow like flowing water. That way you can make your dreams come true. But in this way, the journey of life will also become enjoyable. Keep your thinking clear to others, you can't be good by hurting someone. Let's welcome life by sharing love better than burning in the fire of hatred. Let's start the journey of life with dreams by carving ourselves.

CHAPTER TWO

The Definition of Life

Life is one of the greatest gift of nature. Innumerable lives flourish in the bosom of nature. Each species lives in a limited area to the best of its ability. The most exciting life is that of a human being. Man makes life enjoyable and enjoyable on the basis of his mind and attitude. The existence of evolution is also more possible in human life than others. Life is like running water. It meets with sorrows and joys. But most people forget the waves of happiness and turn the rings of sorrow into a storm. This leaves life as a burden. Your outlook on life is very important. We need to understand that sadness or happiness change like a shadow. No sorrow or happiness lasts too long. They change over time. After defeat, the value of victory is known. We have made life sad and disoriented because of our attitude. The thinking of a sad, directionless life needs to be transformed into a lively life. Stopping to think is a dangerous turn for life. Being sensitive and feeling any emotion change our behavior. We must keep our thinking positive.

Life should be welcomed with smiling faces, without falling into the chains of bigotry and superstition. No one remembers the sad faces, but the feeling of empathy and compassion makes you weaker. Open up your thinking. You will see happiness all around.

You can judge the strength of your point of view from the example of an egg. like as when an external force is felt on an egg, then life ends and if an external

force is felt, then life begins. Similarly, strengthen the strength of your point of view. Keep it up. Because if you tell your sorrows in front of public, everyone

will use their strength to weaken you. If you work on it by understanding the cause of your sorrows then life will start to pass in bliss. Life has three main parts, childhood, youth, old age. Traveling in these areas thinking starts to change. Also, in these parts different religions and social perspectives leave their mark on thinking so it becomes very important to understand them in order to understand life. Life is unique in itself. Be happy to enjoy it. We need to

understand the reality of life. What were your circumstances before you were born and what are your circumstances at death? They all reflect your achievement. We have often read that:

"if you are born poor, you are not at fault but if you are poor at the time of death then you are responsible for this mistake? -Bill Gates

There is a difference between living and cutting life. Sorrow and joy are part of every human being's life and meeting with such life aspects is fixed . The only difference is how we look at them. The way you think, the way you look, give guidance to your life.

People will throw stones at you. This means they will interfere with your work. It is up to you whether you want to build a bridge of these stones or a wall of troubles. Keep thinking positive at all times. Keep trying One day success will kiss your steps. It doesn't matter how many times you lose; it does matter how many times you try to win. As long as you do not accept defeat, no one can defeat you. Learn to live your own life. First of all our steps stop because of the interference of the society. The question arises in our mind what will people say? This fear and question, do not allow our inner skills to become public. As a result, the thinking and customs of the old generation were right at that time but they are not needed now and they have become just superstitions. They also continue from one generation to the next. This is because no one dares to take the initiative. one will have to try to give birth to new customs. These little things make simple and enjoyable life as burden. Keep thinking positive.

Everything will be fine. I am sharing with you an example that will help you to change your negative attitude to a positive one. The scientist who invented the electric bulb, Thomas Edison, failed many times during his research, but one day he succeeded when he did not give up trying. someone asked question to Edison how many times you had failed. What would you like to say about that? Then the scientist replied, "I must have failed in your eyes, but I have succeeded every time." Every time when I failed, I have learned that a revolt can never be formed in this way. If we understand this thinking and have adopted in life, then victory is certain.

"Define life in your own words and look for a purpose in life and pursue goals. "

Childhood

The journey of life begins in childhood. In the beginning, children's minds are is like an empty book. The journey from birth to death begins to write the book of your life. It is in your hands how to write life. What happens around a child during childhood affects his mind. Therefore, it is the parents' responsibility to provide a good environment for their children. Never mention your child's

shortcomings. Try to understand the child's mindset. Parents should show the right way by understanding the hidden art in the children instead of imposing their views on the child by force. If children work hard in a particular field according to their interests, then success will follow in their footsteps. what we learn in childhood we have to pass our whole life under the shadow of that thinking. There are very few people who change their thinking by understanding the passage of time. To understand how childhood events affect the psyche, let's share an example. We often see in society that circus people tie a giant elephant with a chain or rope. The elephant becomes their puppet and makes compromise with time by considering slavery as his life. While he can easily be free. But this thinking is the result of a childhood event. Because when the elephant is small, it is tied with a chain. He constantly strives to be independent but being less powerful in childhood, he cannot do that. Due to which the thing settles in his mind that he cannot break the chain. But when the elephant grows big, it has the ability to break it. But the notion of childhood does not allow him to try. That is why we should never allow misconceptions to develop in children.

Children often learn by imitating their parents. So present yourself the way you want your children to be. Society would be a reflection of the people. People's thinking determines whether society is healthy or weak. The crime rate serves to reflect the mentality of the people. Parents play an important role in a child's development and success. Especially the mother's faith changes the child's life. Let's try to understand this with the help of an example. The great scientist Albert Einstein was expelled from school as a child for being mentally retarded, but his mother gave help to his son to avoid from negative thinking and to be succeed. His mother said, teacher at his school said that your child is smarter than the other children. So it can't read with them properly. Teach him by yourself at home. This boy grew up to be a great scientist. Who made his significant contribution in the field of science. There is no need to panic if a child's thinking is different from the rest of the world. Because often different thinking can bring about development and change. The paths of like-minded people are the same. Crowded roads obstruct access to destinations. Different thinking people construct new roads and crowds follow them. In addition to the parents and the home environment in childhood, there are other important factors that determine the development of children. After home, childhood begins to move towards school, schools work to sharpen your thinking. What is your way of life? It directly or indirectly depends on the thinking of your teacher. So try to give your children good teachers. With the help of education you can eliminate all forms of darkness. Children are the future of the country. So if you want to brighten the future of the country, never compromise with education. Children are able to learn different languages in school. Which further gives them the opportunity to understand and read different cultures, histories and religions. At birth, the child is

just a human form. But soon after birth, he is labelled as caste, religion. Parents should instil humanity in their children, teach them to love others. Tell them about their glorious history. Tell them about every religion, but do not sow the seeds of bigotry and hatred If children understand humanity well then, they will love everyone irrespective of caste, creed, colour. Every religion teaches humanity to love. Love is humanity. The kind of seed that is sown in the child's brain in childhood will bear the same fruit in the future. Childhood is considered a happier time than youth and old age. Because at this time children live a life without any bigotry or negative thinking. The feeling of childhood memories and love helps to give warmth and peace to the rest of life.

"Meet your childhood. Make a list of the dreams that made you happy as a child. Observe the events and accidents that are hindering and encouraging these dreams.

CHAPTER FOUR

Adolescence

After childhood, life meets the second part of adolescence. This is a very important part of life. Because the decision made at this time determines your future. Youth is a very critical turning point. At this time internal and external changes take place. If we make the right decision wisely at this time, then life gets the right path and a small decision taken without thinking can make your life directionless. The future of any country depends on its youth.

Thinking develops during adolescence. Boys and girls lead normal lives. This union gives us a chance to understand each other. This is considered the best time to get married. The companionship of a partner helps to make this life a new beginning of happiness and make the coming journey of life memorable. The relationship on which your future happiness rests should be started wisely. Every parent tries to find a good partner for their children, but there are some things should keep in mind for future happiness.

Child marriage reflects the weak mentality of our society. Depending on the religion, marriage customs may change. But the marriage relationship witness the sweetness of love between two souls. Marriage is mainly divided into two types. Arbitrary marriage and love marriage. Both types have their own advantages and disadvantages. Arbitrary marriage strengthens family ties. But still discrimination of dowry, religion, caste and color, poverty, richness can also be seen in it. This discrimination serves to destroy the sanctity of the relationship. The girls who get married with land and property, their bodies even get married, but their souls are always virgins, tormented and wandering to feel the feeling of love. Marriage and love are both spiritual relationships. By associating them with physical relations we discredit this relationship. Bed sharing and physical contact can meet our physical needs. We can't call it love. It is very important to have love in every

relationship. The love marriage relationship also bears witness to the love affair between two souls. But most boys and girls do not face the reality and inadvertently misrepresent this relationship. As a result, this marriage has to face the opposition of society. This opposition is more prevalent in India. Because here is the bigotry of religion and caste is more. In foreign countries, boys and girls are completely free. It is not necessary for decisions made independently to last too long. There is no place for caste, color or religion in a love marriage. But running away from home and getting married is not solution. It is also important to anticipate the consequences of any action we take. Steps should not be stopped for fear of consequences, but it is important to understand where the steps are taking us. If we understand this then bad results can be turned into good results. The girl who ran away from home and got married may or may not achieve happiness in her life. These joys depend on the sanctity and truth of the relationship. But one wrong step can block the other girls from reading. Unborn baby girls in the womb can be killed. Love marriage cannot be decided right or wrong. Both marriages need improvement. But relationships are linked to wisdom, not rebellion. Rebellion is against one's enemies, not against one's family. This is how we kill happiness and relationships. Happiness is felt only with family. Sacrificing many relationships to protect a relationship is not a wise step. If your relationship is holy and true, then at the right time the family can allow this marriage. If the family still does not agree to the marriage, then you can tell them in clear words, if this relationship of ours becomes an obstacle in the way of your religion, caste and society then we will keep this relationship to ourselves. But we cannot

marry anyone else. Over time, the hot iron also softens. But if your intentions are right. Family support is very important in marriage. On the basis of education, human beings can be divided into three groups. The literate, the less educated and the illiterate each have their own place. Not every literate person is necessarily wise and every illiterate person is a fool. However, when it comes to children getting married, the boy and girl should have the same level and home environment. Because education changes the way we think. Sometimes that thing is too small for one person and too big for another. Being educated is not proof of being wise. Some people are deprived of reading books, they becomes wise on the basis of experience and by reading the book of life . In contrast, some educated people behave like illiterate people. Their certificates, degrees are not proof of education, education is often reflected in your speech and behavior. So it may not apply to everyone. Because the level of understanding and perspective cannot be equal everywhere in terms of education. But still, if we talk on the basis of experience, then the level of thinking of boys and girls must be the same and for the same thinking, the family environment should also have to be the same. For example, households related to agriculture should give priority to girls who know domestic work and working families should give priority to educated girls. No argument can be applied to everyone. But it can help us understand relationships and make decisions. Only when you start relationships with love will love start a new life, to live life understanding is important that make life very simple and enjoyable. we make it a burden ourselves. By changing our way of thinking we can lead to a happier life. The real taste of life is in the sweetness of relationships. But in the blind race of money we are mixing bitterness instead of sweetness in relationships. Today, every relationship begins with a veil of falsehood, whether it is a friendship or something else. In particular, we have made the relationship of marriage as hollow. We make all sorts of compromises to go to abroad. In the past, many people ignored the happiness of their children in the lure of land. But nowadays we ourselves strangle our feelings and desires for the dream of going out. Here IELTS has worked to end gender discrimination against girls, there, the Punjabi nation, known for its honor and dignity, has been taught to compromise for money and dreams like other nations. It is not wrong to marry and go out. But it is completely wrong to do business and demand money only on the basis of

marriage visa. Because dowry in any form will remain a disgrace to the society. It may be appropriate to get married your children for securing their future by sending them abroad. But it is wrong to base the relationship of marriage completely on agreement. Because how it would be fair to deprive those children from choosing their partner or spouse for whom we make compromise and send abroad for securing future. Happiness is not all about money or convenience. Understanding and loyalty to our relationships can also bring happiness. Let's change our thinking to live a better life. In this way you will be able to enjoy a happy season in life. What kind of environment we give to the youth in youth? Its

glimpse is clearly visible in our youth. In foreign developed countries, the youth are given complete freedom. They are not restricted. As a result, these young people work to create a good society and save humanity. On the other hand, in a developing country like India, various restrictions are imposed on the youth. As a result, young people deviate from the right path and choose the path of crime. To

realize this difference, we can compare crimes like rape between foreign countries and India. This is the truth; it cannot be ignored. But this does not mean that all Indians have bad thinking. But in terms of numbers, India is one of them where such type of

incidents and crime are more common. At this age, youth are victims of crime and drugs. If the youth get proper education and become a part of jobs and business, then the future of the country is secured. At the same time, education helps young people deepen their culture and language. Every country gives a different environment to the youth of his country. So we can say that people in different parts of the world live differently. In foreign countries, children are completely free. As adults, they struggle for their own future. They make their own decisions about life. Everything has two or more aspects. In the same way one should know the good and bad aspects of this environment of complete freedom. This environment makes children more responsible and responsible decision makers. They try to fulfill their dreams by working on their own thinking without any interference. But because of this freedom, children do not care about their parents and parents do not care about their children. In this way the lack of mutual love can be felt in their relationship. Adulthood is the right time to make life decisions. Young people can make their own decisions. But if they share their decisions with their parents, the parents help them make the right decision based on their life experiences. Everything is bound to change over time. But there is no age of experience. In this way young people avoid the failures that their parents have faced at their age. On the other hand, in a country like India, even after reaching adulthood, most decisions are made by the parents. like this

mutual love becomes strong in the family. This mutual bond helps to preserve our mother tongue, culture and dress. Because a glimpse of your father's, grandfather's time and the warmth of love can be easily enjoyed through it. Depending on the parents, young people are somewhat slow in understanding their responsibilities and becoming capable of them. Because every responsibility is realized by taking responsibility. There is as much difference between thinking and doing as there is between dream and reality.

"If you want kids to keep their feet on the ground, put some responsibility on their shoulders - Pauline Phillips.

If kids have a strong grip on the ground, they can start flying. After this discussion, it becomes

imperative that the question arises in the minds of all that the way of life of foreign countries and countries like India is different but they also have their own disadvantages and advantages. Then what is the best way to live a good, happy life? In every country, religion and culture there are both good and evil. So no single method can be completely right for our life. Because even with a single thought, our life will come to a standstill. Staying means you will be limited to a circle, a boundary. Even standing water gets dirty. So let the flow of thought flow like water. Every religion, culture and country should be brought together to create a common way of life. Continue the journey of youth till old age by living every moment in a good

way. Because sorrow and happiness are part of life , after one part of life another will be waiting for you. If worrying puts an end to suffering, worry. If anxiety is robbing your happiness, leave it behind and move on. Set a goal in your life and keep

working hard. One day success will kiss your steps.

"Work to learn in youth, not to earn - Robert Kiosky

"Try to understand whether the dreams taken in childhood turned into youth or not. what were the steps for your dreams and Find out the reasons for successes and failures.

CHAPTER FIVE

Old age

Old age is the last part of life. This journey of life starts from birth and pass through young and old age finally ends by meeting death. This journey is not complete for everyone. Because many people fall into the clouds of death in childhood or adolescence due to natural or unnatural causes. In old age, human beings derive the essence of life based on their experience. Money or other benefits do not matter to them at this time. For them, children's love and family happiness are everything. They feel that they have wasted precious time in the cycle of making the future happy since childhood. At this time one realizes the importance of happiness and ourselves. The joy and comfort that comes from spending time with your spouse and grandchildren in old age cannot be described in words. In the past time , people lived in joint families, especially in India. Where children were loved by their grandparents. With the help of children, old age passes easily. It does not allow the elderly to feel lonely. But due to some other reasons and influence of Western culture, joint families became single families. As a result, children are deprived of the love of their grandparents. Always less importance and time is given to old ones by adolescence . As a result old age starts to lost in the clouds of loneliness where the peers whom with, they share their sorrows and joys are reduced. That's why young people need to spend some time each day with the elderly . So that they can feel happy even on their last journey. The way children and the elderly think changes over time. As a result, the distance between the thoughts of both overwhelms on the sweetness of the relationship. That is why elders need to keep trying to change over time. Anyway, life at this age teaches patience. Understand each other together and end the last journey with a smiling face. When life ends, your character should become a flame of happiness and realize your victory to the darkness of sadness .

Knowing a little about the setting of sun, means does not detract the importance of thrill. "Carl Sagan"

"Remember your past life. Make a list of these good and bad memories separately. Calm down with good memories. Share the bad experiences that got from bad memories with new generation.

CHAPTER SIX

Religion

The greatest religion of life is humanity, with the help of which human beings meet each other with a feeling of love. An example of humanity is set by helping one another in times of sorrow and happiness. Man has deviated from his true religion and has been divided into other religions. All religions teach man to love humanity. According to one's own thinking and point of view, the message of religion and religious texts is worship able for some and understandable for others. The world is very unique and vast in itself. Different religions are prevalent in different countries. Religions change from time to time. Talking about all religions is not the subject of this book. Because there are so many religions but their destination is the same, to tell man the way of life so that the existence of humanity can testify to love. In the world, Aryan, Roman religion, Sikhism, Hinduism, Jainism, Buddhism, Zoroastrianism, Chinese religion, Japanese religion, Judaism, Christianity, Marxism, Islam and many other religions are considered. Citizens of progressive countries like Canada, USA try to understand all religions and change accordingly. Their thinking is not limited to any one religion. They understand religion on the basis of scientific truth and incorporate it into their lives. That is why we see less fanaticism, hatred and negative thinking in them than in other countries. They do not associate food and clothing with religion. Perhaps there is no

hypocrisy on the name of religion. India, on the other hand, is known as a secular country. Here Hindus, Sikhs, Muslims and people of many other religions are living their lives freely according to their religion. Gurus belonging to different religions were born on this earth and wrote religious texts. Only those who put humanity first can be religious.

Sikhism tells the way of living life heartly. In other words, we can say that Sikhism is the only religion that teaches man the lesson of humanity. Reading the Sikh Guru Granth Sahib Ji, the religious scripture of the Sikhs, brings a different kind of joy and peace of living one's life accordingly. Let us read the views of two scholars on this subject.

"All religious granths has read but peace to mind and brain that has met from reading Sikh's granth sahib never met from any other granth sahib". Pearl S. Bank

1. "Sikhs are also to blame for the message of Sikhism not reaching the world. No one else, Sikhism is not the property of Sikhs but it came into existence for the betterment of all humanity."- Bertrand Russell

2. If you want to live your life happily then move forward by good understanding of the religious aspect. Because with the help of religion, it becomes easier to walk on the path of humanity. Sad life has a reason to be happy. But that does not mean that your happiness depends on religion.

Religion is only a means and support. Your happiness depends on your thinking. Look around you some believers will meet you miserable, on the other hand some will meet you happy despite being an atheist. We don't need to be confused with the existence of God, just find the real reason for happiness.

"Question your religion, apply its teachings in your
personal life. Make a list of the facts for humanity that
stand in the way of religion and hope. Start working on
expectations and understand the

hypocrisy inside the barriers and separate yourself from
the sheep."

CHAPTER SEVEN

Family Relationships

Family relationships play a very important role in our lives. Your honesty regarding relationships make your relationship legitimate and illegitimate. Often in society the offspring born out of a relationship established only for the fulfillment of physical relations is called illegitimate. Not illegitimate offspring but illegitimate relationship. Motherhood is never illegitimate, but your thinking put the question of illicit relationships in question. The relationships that we hide from the society are

illegitimate, legitimate relationships are open in the society. If you have strong family relationships and they have faith, the sweetness of love, so you can live your life happily as compared to others whose family relationships are weak. There will be ups and downs in your life. If your family is with you, you can enjoy your all Happiness in the fullest way. Happiness without oneself seems artificial. Family support makes you strong in both happiness and sorrow. Because there is a reason for sorrow and failure.

Other people only see your failures and question on your abilities according to their own thinking. This attitude weakens you. You may find yourself in the thick darkness of sadness. If the family is with you, the views of others will not matter to you. When you share your grief with someone, the griefs are gone. From this conversation you can see the way forward. So be honest with your family relationships. Set boundaries for family relationships based on your experience. Just because all relatives and family

members may not understand you well does not mean that only blood relatives can be family

members. Those who understand you and you have more trust on them than oneself can become your

family. It is necessary for you have such few special relatives in your life. With whom you can share everything. The understanding of relationships varies. This difference can also be found in the thinking of men and women. Loyalty is very

important in every relationship. Parents need to build strong friendships with their children. So that they can tell their parents about their life and what their dreams are. What obstacles are they experiencing in their dreams? That way they will start taking steps towards a better life. Appreciate your parents, take some time out of your daily life for them so that you can listen to their experiences. Everyone thinks positively about your life, but no one can think better for you than your parents. All other relationships are connected with the relationship of husband and wife. It is also the responsibility of the parents to show the children the right path and make their dreams come true. Only a good son and daughter-in-law can take care of their elderly parents, if their relationship will strong and comfortable then they will be able to handle all other relationships easily. So we must understand that having a strong

family relationship in your family is very important for a good life.

"Think about the relationships that are of special importance in your life. Try to know the nature, dreams of each member to strengthen the grip of happiness in these relationships. Make a list of weaknesses and try your best to overcome them."

The Importance of Women in Life

Women play a very important role in life. Because life begins through woman. The journey from one generation to another is not possible without a woman. Life does not only mean breathing; it also means maintaining relationships and feeling happy. Whatever the relationship, a woman's attachment to that relationship makes that relationship important. It would probably not be wrong to call a woman life.

It would be very important to understand the

mentality of a woman. But in every relationship, most people try to explain the woman instead of understanding her. According to every relationship, a woman's thinking changes. Naturally, this change is also seen in men. But most people look at a woman

with the same eyes. The main basis of this vision is physical attraction. Social relationships are born out of a woman's womb. Woman is a form of power, patience and renunciation. Although India has become independent, it is sad to say that women are still slaves here. She realizes this slavery from the narrow mindedness of the society. The patriarchal country tries to hide its weaknesses by imprisoning women in chains of slavery. A woman expects respect, but somewhere she does not get the respect she deserves. Oppression against women is on the rise. This is due to the narrow and lustful thinking of men. The condition of the society and the standard of prices is going down to a very low level. The woman herself is feeling insecure everywhere, whether it's city streets or a village fair, or an office. Girls are outperforming boys in every sector by reading and writing. Now we need to unite for our own identity and dignity and overcome the narrow mindedness of the society. The kind of behavior and respect we expect from people for our mothers, sisters, can't we give this respect to every woman. if boy tease a girl, then a girl is restricted to go out from home, in fact there is need to control boy not to let him go openly. A girl can sit at home, but she will be replaced by another victim. If you are fond of asking for dowry

from your daughter in laws then have the courage to

give dowry to your daughters. Every ritual should be viewed from the same point of view. For a girl, her dowry should be given to her as an honor. A decision made with discrimination can only satisfy our narrow mindedness. But it will lead the society to decline. Nothing in society is stable and sustainable. It needs to change from time to time. It depends on our thinking whether we are moving society in the right direction or in the wrong direction. We need a time when girls, like boys, can make their own decisions. To some extent, this change has begun. In our society, girls are made to feel inferior from childhood, which is directly or indirectly weakening women. If we sow the seeds of healthy thinking then in a good society our daughters and sisters will be able to breathe in the open air. We need to elevate the character of the turban again so that even the most insecure place feels safe when we see the

sardars. we don't know how many generations we have spent in explaining to a woman, can we dedicate a generation to understand woman. Understanding a woman requires an understanding of each

relationship. Every understanding creates a passion for happiness and success in you.

"you take the first step towards success only when you think about getting out of the current environment?" -Mark Kane

Life begins with a mother's relationship. First of all we need to understand this relationship. Mother is the form of God, not God. Only the mother can take the initiative to compromise and sacrifice for the

happiness of the children. All relationships arc important in their own right but above all is the

mother's relationship. A man does not leave any step to make woman weak and feel her inferior but when they will realize that a woman who is in pain during childbirth can never be weak. If weak then man's thinking.

The following lines express this woman's physical pain beautifully:

"It is not easy to hear the squeaking of child , the woman puts her life on the palm to call herself a mother." Davinder Varma

Changing thinking only for one day can't prove you good, it cannot be anything without a show off. Just being imbued with mother's affection on Mother's Day and looking at a woman with a weak mentality during the rest of the days proves that we are becoming good for showing off. Often the values in the society are falling. On a religious day we become religious. On Mother's Day our affection awakens.

Do we have respect for our mother every day in life? Does our head bow at the feet of the mother or not? The day we get the answers to these questions. Probably showing off will end and turn in reality. A mother can raise a son or a daughter by starving, lying in a wet place, so why is it difficult for all the children to raise a mother in old age. If Motherhood is to be seen or felt then it can be seen not only in human beings but also in animals. Change is a law of nature. This change has changed the thinking of today's woman. Today's woman is not confined to the house and is also working shoulder to shoulder with the man. She has proved her power by working with men. But still the mother did not give up the

responsibility of taking care of the child. Along with work, raising children is still a part of motherhood. let's assume that only the mother of the children can understand some of the needs. But isn't it the right of a man to give up narrow mindedness and respect a

woman and be a part of her responsibility? Often, we learn what is happening around us is part of our society. But have we ever wondered where we learn to scratch or stare at a woman's breast when we grow up drinking the breast milk of a mother? It was not part of our society. We need to change our thinking.

Its standard has to be raised. Women should be respected. That woman be in any form of

relationship. She will definitely become someone's mother one day. If a woman is pushed in front of our eyes in the society, then if we help her in that woman without seeing our own, stranger then we can call this society a healthy society. Let's change our thinking towards women.

Only respecting her can really explain the meaning of Mother's Day. The day old age homes will disappear from our society. The existence of God Will be established in every home. Rape will stop, women will be able to breathe in the open air everywhere without seeing the difference

between day and night. On that day we will be able to celebrate Mother's Day. Let's eradicate hypocrisy and create a society where women are not exploited but respected. People can complete the journey of seeing God from their mother instead of seeking God in religious places. Your thinking is your shadow.

Eliminate the shadow of this weak thinking, it can only be started by leaving the shadow behind. Let's start with good thinking and good steps.

"Keep your face towards the sun, the shadows will follow you" - Walt Whitman

After the mother, the woman maintains the

relationship of wife and friend as well as many other relationships. She should be given desired respect after understanding the importance of every

relationship . It is also the brother's duty to help his sister fulfill her dreams. If he presents his new ideas in the right way, families can give equal freedom to both boys and girls without discrimination.

Understanding your wife is also a very important step in the sweetness of family relationships. Because she can leave her home, family for you. There is no need to tell her how much your happiness means to her.

She should be given a good environment. If the

relationship between you and your spouse is strong. You will be able to handle other relationships easily. Like every relationship, friendship is very important for a woman. For friendship, it doesn't matter if it is a boy or a girl. But still the atmosphere in a country like India is not completely conducive to boy-girl

friendship. Such a society can only create new thinking. Society is formed because of people; people are not formed because of society. Good society or bad society depends on our thinking. We need some customs to walk in the society. These customs can vary depending on the religion, culture and caste.

But its basic purpose is the same. We have to

maintain social relations to manage the activities of the society from generation to generation. These

relationships are also incomplete without a woman and it becomes necessary to have a woman to continue the journey from generation to generation. These relationships are either related by blood, for example grandparents, parents, siblings or trying to weave religion, caste, culture into a common thread of relationships gives birth to relationships. Out of

which many relationships like husband-wife, brother-in-law, sister-in-law are born. All of these

relationships are important in themselves. It maintains communal harmony. The journey of

human life in the society continues smoothly. There is a different kind of relationship than all other

relationships. The sacred bond of friendship, which is based on strong aspects like humanity, trust,

respect for each other. This relationship is far above caste and religious bigotry and is a sacred

relationship, which only teaches love to humanity.

People of any religion or special caste cannot be bad but the bad thinking of some bad people divides people and turns them into a hateful society. Where our thinking towards other castes and other religions falls to a very low level. It is no less than a cancer for our society. So the only solution to this disease is

friendship, the message of love. With its help, we can save humanity from dying. Also, society can be prevented to become hollow based on caste worms. Friendships also have to deal with bigotry in society.

As a result, an attempt is made to present a negative image of this relationship in the society. A friendship is a relationship in which we can share everything

with our friends and find a solution to the problem.

We feel more secure when we share things with a friend than we do with a parent or a spouse.

Friendships can be made with people of another race, religion, or opposite sex. Which is the backbone of

unity and humanity. Friendship has no age. An old man can be friends with a child, a child with a young man and a boy with a girl. To some extent, society accepts the friendship between race and religion. But the anti-social sex can't tolerate a girl's friendship

with a boy. We all know that the constant journey

from one generation to another is possible only with the combination of man and woman. As a result, physical relationships are created in the relationship.

Attraction to each other is natural due to nature. But it has nothing to do with friendship because

friendship is in two thoughts and ideas, not two bodies. Boys and girls can understand each other in better way with the help of friendship. As a result, other relationships are stronger, because their

foundation is laid with friendship, love, in which no weak foundation of caste and religious bigotry is possible. We also cannot ignore the fact that some inferior types of people try to play with bodies and dignity by wearing the masks of friendship. Who try unsuccessfully to obscure the sanctity of friendship. We have to understand that such bad games are played in other relationships even without

friendship. Then why we do protest against

friendship? We need a good society and a free air environment where bad relationships can be

created. This is possible only if the roots of the sacred bond of friendship can be deepened. Friendship is

only the way with its help we can understand each

other , after spending some time with that person the difference between fake and actual face can be

understood. Let's try to create a healthy society with the help of a sacred relationship like friendship. This journey will start from friendship and the rest of the relationships will also be colored in the color of

friendship. with it every child be friend of parents and share every matter. In this way evils can be eradicated from society. With the thread of

friendship we can weave all relationships into the garland of humanity. If the woman is happy in every relationship, then the relationship will also be strong.

"Understand the role of a woman in your life. Give name to the relationships of the women in your life.

Discuss your thoughts regarding them. Correct mistakes by acknowledging.

CHAPTER NINE

Criticism give birth to development

Life is a continuous journey of victories and defeats. Every step of it proves to be helpful in meeting you with some or the other feeling. You just need to

change the way of thinking and higher up. In order to live in the society we have to face the society, this encounter will be in the form of your praise or your criticism. Honest thinking and faith in your work is enough to make you successful. What people will say, don't be afraid of people's criticism. Negative aspects like criticism, hatred are the product of development. Patience and humility are declining day by day.

Hatred is growing in the society. How we move

forward, our focus is not more on this, we trying to

stop someone else from moving forward. Opposition and criticism help in development. Because the more there is opposition to something, the more people are curious about it. Criticism or taunting from someone can encourage you to move forward or break you

from within. It's up to you, how you look at it. This criticism is like a stone that people will keep throwing in your way. It depends on your thinking that from these stones you build a wall of troubles or a bridge to success. There is no doubt that criticism breeds

growth. But it still needs to end. Yet somewhere this feeling of criticism and hatred is a stigma on our

society. That is why our identity becomes

misrepresented in front of people automatically. We all will have to make an effort to eradicate these evils from the society. Criticism can be humbly based on an argument. But by protesting through nonsense talks we only try to quell the fire of our hatred which has a very bad effect on our society. Criticism can break someone's morale and stop them from moving forward. Because not everyone's viewpoint is strong and accurate. Only then the seed of positive thinking can germinate in the society. If we will eliminate the pollution of criticism. There is a difference in thinking between us and foreigners, which make us apart from each other. For example, we can see

white people when they see a disabled person sitting on a wheelchair, they show a slight smile and move forward. Whatever is in their heart but this slight

smile becomes a cause of happiness. It is no less than a praise for him. But on the other hand our people keep turning their heads towards the helpless person even if they move forward. Their way of looking makes them feel inferior. By doing negative talks in front of the miserable person, we weaken him and make him character of sympathy. Instead of learning the wrong things from Western culture, let's learn

some good things. Which can help strengthen our

society. There is no discrimination between boys and girls in abroad. Or there is no suffocation in the air

so there are very few rapes than us. There is no tradition of worshiping rivers and oceans like we do, perhaps that is why the rivers there are clean. How long will we continue to sink into the mire of criticism? These improvements we have to do for our society, for the future of the next generation. Let us preserve our culture and make the good habits of

other civilizations, good thinking a part of our thinking. As a result our children will be able to avoid hateful, critical thinking in the future. They will choose the right path and work hard to move

forward. Those who

are troubled by criticism never succeed. If you have set a goal in your life, keep working hard and one day you will succeed. The negative attitude of people towards you does not weaken you, but you can work harder than before to establish your abilities. By the way, it is not important to prove your ability. You

have to believe in yourself. But sometimes life brings you to a point where you break from within and become as silent as a calm ocean. Let us understand an example to understand this. "Once in the United States, there was an attempt to make a lion race with dogs, the dogs made a lot of noise, hungry but the lion sat quietly. The race started; the dogs ran with full

force but the lion did not move from its place. The mental state of the lion was studied and a summary

was drawn, the lion thought that I know my instincts, I do not need to prove anything by running with the dogs, the conclusion - do not argue unnecessarily

with anyone, if you are able, you do not need to tell, don't compete with someone to raise their height,

your silence becomes an embarrassing answer for that person who is in front of you but it is only for those who feel ashamed not for those who do not feel ashamed. If you want to compete, do it with yourself and not with others. Also take a negative view of people in a positive way. In this way criticism will

help you to strengthen you instead of weakening. Criticism, although it produces development, we must stop opposing someone by burning our hatred. Let's

start thinking about your own life and stop

interfering in other people's lives. Let's get rid of what people think of us and make it clear what we think about our lives. If life and happiness are ours, then

we also have the right to think about it and fulfill life's dreams. So let us work hard to set our own limits of happiness. Fate and negative thinking of people cannot defeat you unless you accept defeat in your life. With hard work we can also change the lines of destiny. People who blame fate often find excuses to avoid their responsibilities. In society, we often find that people decide themselves about hard work and skills of others that they cannot do this. If we can't encourage someone then we have no right to break their morale. Rather than regretting for those decisions that take in hurry, try to bring coolness in nature so that we can change our way of thinking

with the pace of life and become bold and positive. we need to learn the skill of making decisions with patience and wisdom about the decisions on which our happiness rests. With this step, let's try to create a healthy society by making a fresh start in life, so that our future generation will be free from hatred.

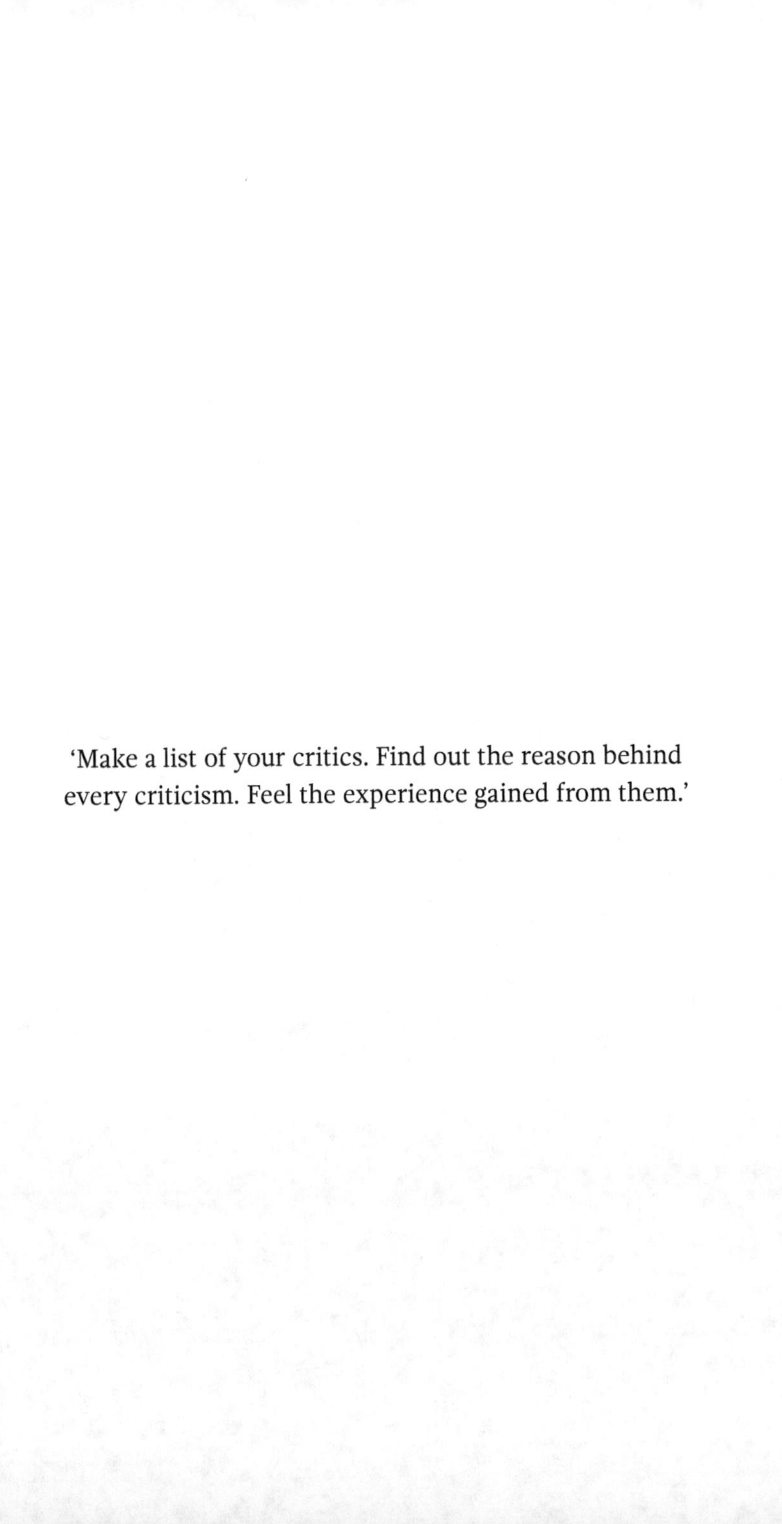

'Make a list of your critics. Find out the reason behind every criticism. Feel the experience gained from them.'

CHAPTER TEN

Believe in your skills and hard work

It is very important to believe in yourself to create happiness in life. Without faith everything else

becomes meaningless. Happiness and sorrow depend on your attitude. Helping others can be a strength to you, but don't let it become your weakness. No one can fully understand your difficulties and obstacles without you. So start working on yourself for your dreams and happiness.

"Eat well, read books, read yourself, develop your mind, do good and become good. Last but not least,

remember that your most important investment is in yourself - Warren Buffett.

First of all, let your thoughts fly in the sky of ideas.

Through this flight you can see dreams based on your hobbies and happiness. Give the dream a goal and purpose to achieve the dream, try to implement constructive thinking by turning the plan into action to achieve the goal.

"Imagination often takes us into a world that never happens but without it we can't go anywhere - Carl Sagan"

The human mind can imagine and believe . Also, it can even get him - Napoleon Hill

So start dreaming. Hope and the desire to know something create new paths. New paths lead to sorrows as well as new joys. Every victory and

success is born from the womb of dreams. Victories and defeats go hand in hand, but never let unfulfilled dreams overwhelm your happiness. Fight hard in life without despair, keep working hard. One day you

will reach your destination. Getting Victory without suffering sorrows and obstacles can't make you happier. Never let your dreams die.

"The most dangerous is to be filled with peace of the dead, to endure everything despite not having the

strength to endure the pain, to leave home for work and to return home from work, the most dangerous is the death of our dreams." Avtar Singh Pash

Let's build faith in our dreams before we die. Let's try to understand a story to understand the power of faith. Sylvester Stallone is a well-known and wealthy American actor in Hollywood. He had set a milestone in the world of acting with a film like Rocky. He has

so much wealth today that he can split it with both hands or burn notes but it will not finish. This is

from the days when Solvent Stallone was going through a period of economic slavery. He also had to steal and sell his wife's jewelry due to financial difficulties. Sylvester Stallone's financial situation

was going to deteriorate with day . The condition had reached to sell the house and become homeless. After losing his house, he had to spend three nights

sleeping at a bus stop in New York. He did not have the means to rent a room at that time, nor did he have any money in his pocket to buy something to eat. In such a situation Salvasser Stallone tried to sell his pet dog to a stranger in front of a liquor store because he did not have the money to please the dog. Sylvester Stallone sold the dog he loved so much for twenty-five dollars and left crying. Two weeks later, Sylvester Stallone watched a boxing match between Homat Ali and Chuck Weppner, and has get inspired for the script of Rocky movie. Sylvester Stallone

spent a full twenty hours writing the script for the Rocky movie. Sylvester Stallone approached the filmmakers to sell the story and they have offered

$25,000. But the mess came when Sylvester Stallone made it a condition for Rocky to play the lead role in the film. The producer replied that he would make a film with an established actor. He mocked Sylvester Stallone. That you just look like a jhudu! Sylvester Stallone returned disrespectfully, picking up his

script. A few weeks later, Sylvester Stallone was approached by people from the same producer's

studio and offered $ 250,000, asking him to give up acting. Sylvester Stallone turned down the offer. He increased the amount to$ 50,000. Sylvester Stallone

also turned him down and said that he would play the lead role himself. Tired, he finally agreed to take

Sylvester Stallone as main character in movie. But he reduced the price of the script to just $ 35,000.

Sylvester Stallone immediately agreed. From that day onwards, poverty became a thing of the past for

Sylvester Stallone. When the Rocky film reached the masses, it broke many film records and won many Oscars that year. Sylvester Stallone was announced the best character for rocky movie. Rocky movie was also voted the best Hollywood film of all time by the American national film industry. With a salary of

$35,000 from the filmmaker, Sylvester first tried to get his dog back. The store in front of which Salvasser Stallone sold the dog. He went there and waited for three days for a man to whom he sold the dog. On the third day, the man was seen carrying a dog to Sylvester Stallone. Sylvester Stallone's eyes

sparkled. Sylvester Stallone requested to him for

getting dog back by telling him the reason of selling. Sylvester Stallone offered a hundred dollars to buy dog that he sold for twenty-five dollars. The dog's

owner refused. Sylvester Stallone offered five

hundred dollars. The dog's owner refused again.

Sylvester Stallone offered a thousand dollars. The dog's owner refused it again. Increasing the amount, the owner turned down the offer of ten thousand dollars, saying that when you sold the dog, it was for sale. Not for sale now. In the end, the dog, sold for five dollars, was bought back by Sylvester Stallone for fifteen thousand dollars. When Salvasser Stallone

was going back after buying the dog, seller stopped

him and asked why you spent so much money to buy this dog. Sylvester Stallone replied with a laugh, "I

used to share my grief with dog when I fell down exhausted from suffering from poverty. I could bear my hunger. But my dog could not stand hunger. So he would smash things around and find something to eat. I learned a lesson from my dog we should never sit empty by giving up. Keep hitting your hands and feet, sometimes your paw will get stuck somewhere.

That's what I did and now I'm a Hollywood star. The results that you get after each victory and defeat hone your thinking. Sitting helpless in the face of storms can be nothing more than suicide and weakness. So keep doing something without getting tired.

Dreaming while sleeping is like standing at one position and something that stands cannot develop. See dreams with open eyes, the fire of passion burning inside you will not allow you to stop and

sleep. Learn from your mistakes how to make up your shortcomings.

"Spending life by making mistakes is more honorable than staying free"

George Bernard Shaw.

Get out from your house and safety. Just like boats are safest on shore but they are not built for this purpose. People who are victims of darkness do not stop leaving their homes, only if they will take the

risk they will meet success. There is nothing wrong with making a mistake, without learning something from that mistake, repeating mistakes again is called a sin. Look around you or the world, you will never find a person like this who has never done anything wrong. As you experience the stumbling block, this experience will strengthen the grip of your steps.

Strong things never produce weak results, the absence of weakness welcomes the presence of happiness.

"Recognize your hidden talents. Make a list of your qualities, identify the most appropriate ones that are essential to your dreams. Start carving them with

hard work and experience.

CHAPTER ELEVEN

Create Happiness Better Than Waiting

The definition of happiness needs to be understood.

Until we do not know the true meaning of an emotion or a feeling, till that time we can't feel them properly. Not every laughing face is happy and not every happy face laughs. Happiness can be called 'a kind of

mental stay'. In fact, your level of thinking is the basis of your happiness. place winners in any field do not happy and on the contrary the second or third place winners have not limit of happiness. It is clear that happiness has no limits, but your thinking sets boundaries. Feel every little happiness instead of running after great happiness.

"If you don't have time for the little things, you will not have time for the big things." - Richard Branson

" The journey of hundred miles starts with one step."

Happiness can be begun with dreaming.

Let's start happiness with small joys and dreams. We don't even know when these joys will great. Enjoy every day and moment of life openly thinking that this is your last day. Before going to bed at night, have peace in my heart, whether I see tomorrow's sunrise or not, there will be a look of happiness on my face.

There are hidden sorrows in the past in everyone's life, in the grip of which the joys of our future are bound, like the joys of the face of a poor man bound with compulsion. So take lessons from the past, take courage and fly in the sky of happiness like a free bird.

"You can't plan for the future with the past. Edmund Burke

Old stumbles and wounds will not set us free unless we understand the difference between hotness and warmth. Save the past only in your memories but never try to save the past. If we can change an accident by thinking about the past, then there is the benefit of thinking. If this past is destroying both our

present and future by giving darkness of sorrows that

never ends, then we have to light a new dream and passion within ourselves. With this the dark night of sorrows will end and the morning of happiness will be born. The defeat of your life does not end your life but inspires you to make a fresh start.

"There is no need to stress about the problem we can solve, on the contrary there is no need to stress about the problem we can't solve." - Adolf Hitler

Walking on old roads will make you a victim of crowds. Running after someone else's happiness, you will lose your desires. So learn to live for yourself,

happiness will automatically become your shadow. Dare to walk on different paths with different thinking. May these paths lead to your happiness. You will not meet crowds on these roads. This will allow

you to avoid the interference of others. You will be able to focus on your happiness.

"Every bird finds shelter during the rain, but the eagle flies over the clouds to avoid the rain. "A. P. J. Abdul Kalam

So never seek help in the clouds of misery like
helpless birds. Take courage to fly above the clouds.
Happiness will make you feel lighter and something lighter
often gets up. Expecting something from
someone and depending on him means to put one's
own happiness with own hands in the cage of slavery.

Never expect anything from anyone, start living life in
such a way that you become hope for people.

"Find out the cause of your sorrows and joys. Work on the aspects that hinder them. Think positive and start doing good to create new happiness. "

CHAPTER TWELVE

Appreciate Time

Time is the most important part of life. Without it, happiness and sorrow cannot be felt well. So never

waste your precious time on useless works. If you will waste time, one day time will waste you. Every

happiness and sorrow can be realized at the right time. The meaning of happiness changes by over time. Sometimes we work full time to become financially strong. As a result, family relationships tend to weaken due to lack of time. So we can't call working all the time punctual. This means that we must use our time wisely. Divide the time according to your dreams and daily activities. If every task is given the right timing, then the result will be very

good. Because your every work will be on time. Your focus on one task at a time, the results are likely to be better than expected. Sometimes we give time to more than one task without any thought and as a

result the result has to be affected. Because you are doing something else and your focus is somewhere else. This habit is an obstacle to your success. At the same time your time would be wasted. This wasted time will plunge you into a whirlwind. It will ruin

your happiness.

Doing respect of time include in your children habit. Because childhood is the right time for everything like as at that time the child's mind is like a blank

sheet of paper. The way you write on it will become a habit of the child in the life to come. Waiting for

someone is considered to be the most difficult task. if you promise to meet someone at a certain time, you should arrive at that time. But most people do not arrive on time. Let's change ourselves instead of

wasting our time trying to change someone else.

Recognize the value of your time and go to work on time even if the other partner doesn't come. This may make your partner feel bad at first but this step of

yours can help him to be punctual. Because he will value your time as well as the fear of not arriving on time will make him punctual. If we wait for someone to be late. Then he will value your time. So it's up to you how you view life. If you want to fill life with

happiness, then valuing time will be the key to

happiness for you. So never think that your small mistakes will affect your life and happiness. The

secret of every success and failure is hidden in these tiny habits. Make yourself worthy that after the

setting of the sun you should be awake to welcome the moon and you have to be the witness of the rising of the sun at the setting of the moon. Because if you learn to walk in the footsteps of nature then nature will help you to reach the destination of success and happiness. If you do not live your life according to nature then you may have to pay the price by

sacrificing your happiness. Every second is important for a working person. Day and night, months, years seem to him smaller than his dreams. On the contrary, a person who is idle all the time would feel useless every second and even bigger. It would be difficult for him to spend the day. This restlessness affects his attention. As a result, he begins to cut his life instead of living.

"Run if you can't fly, walk if you can't run, if you can't walk then crawl - But keep walking always.

Martin Luther King, Junior"

Wake up and don't stop until the goal is achieved" -

Swami Vivekananda Swami

Vivekananda's statement motivates us to value time wisely. This does not mean that we can be happier or more successful by working consistently. Because it doesn't matter how much time you work, but it does matter how much time you work properly. In wrong direction and doing work without planning constantly is equal to waste time. In this way you

start living a life and you become a victim of sorrow and sadness. But you've got to enjoy life and start painting it in the colors of prosperity. Donkey can also work continuously that you can ready yourself to live life as slave as donkey. If not, then compare yourself to a good quality instead of a donkey. Try to understand your time in detail from all angles. our time is divided into three parts. The first is the past tense, the

second is the present, and the third is the future.

Each part is important in itself. But the whole game of life depends on the running time. Because we cannot change the past. So it would be good to forget the accidents that happened in the old life. Even your good memories are attached with that time. But never give your memories the right to ruin your present and future. It is wise to make memories the warmth of feelings and learn from accidents that will

bring peace in your future life. If you get caught up in the grip of memories, this warmth will turn into heat

. Heat will destroy your dreams. So focus on the

running time. Create good memories and happiness at this time. This will one day become your past, a past that will have warmth and peace in its bosom.

The work done in the present not only illuminates the past but also works to remove the darkness of the

future. Because the end of darkness can be started with a small lamp. It depends on your hard work

whether this lamp will become the sun or the victim of wind in the future. Therefore, in addition to producing light, it is important to increase the light and shorten the lifespan of the darkness. All these qualities will prove your grip on the present moment.

Never loosen the grip too much so that the door of your dreams slips from your hands. Do not tighten the grip too much as it may break. Mold your work into the structure of hard work according to your dreams. Everything else you will learn over time.

"Divide the time according to your dreams. Make a list of the most important dreams by writing them on top and others write in descending order as needed. Divide the time according to their need.

CHAPTER THIRTEEN

Learn to take decisions

Life is a beautiful journey. Which starts from birth named station. This journey passes through childhood, adolescence, and ends at old age.

Happiness and sorrow travel as passengers during this journey. Every happiness and sorrow passes with the passage of time. This time gives us

experience. Decision need to be taken in every step of life. Initially, parents take decisions for their children. Children are educated on the basis of this decision. After getting education , children become able to take their own decisions. But sometimes life brings us on such turn where we cannot take decision. There could be more than one reason behind the confusion of not taking this decision. Just like the memories associated with the past never allow us to make a decision contrary to the past.

Sometimes the fear of the result of a decision prevents us from making a decision. Our helplessness works as trouble for us, along with it, it wastes our time and we have to pay the cost of decision that we have not taken at right time. Delaying this decision

may put your happiness today and tomorrow at stake.

So learn to take decisions. Every decision should be made on the basis of one's own understanding and experience. But it is important to seek the opinion of your parents and friends. If you feel you have to decide on a particular topic or area and your parents and friends don't know about it, you can seek the advice of another expert in the field. Every human being has different circumstances.

As a result, the outcome of each decision is different. Still, much can be learned from experience.

"Experience is the only source of knowledge" - Albert Einstein

If with the help of experience you will become completely known about that field then adapt these nuances to build new structure based on your hard

work and circumstances. Haste and delay in making a decision both harmful. Because success and

happiness come from working hard at the right time.

Yields can never be expected from unseasonal and uncultivated crops. Doing so wastes our time and brings disappointment instead of experience. So have the courage to make the right decision at the right time. The seed of every success and happiness can

germinate from the land of self-confidence. Realize your qualities and skills. Ignoring weaknesses does not mean careless from them. The only reason is to never let weaknesses overwhelm your skills and

strengths. Self-confidence is the name of a great power. When we realize this power and start taking steps based on it then success and happiness start

moving towards us. Without self confidence we fall prey to rumors. There must be a reason behind every failure. Rumors do not allow us to focus on that cause. As a result, we deviate from our goal. If your thinking and circumstances are different from people's then you also learn to differentiate people's rumors. It takes time to affect good thing on us but bad and negative things affect quickly. Educate

yourself to build self-confidence. Because education is the root of all weaknesses and failures. Whether you know about a field or not, if you know how to read and write, you can get information about any field.

Even illiterate people can gather this information. But they may get incomplete information. Or they may not understand the information as well as you do. You must have a desire to learn something new. This desire can answer all your questions. Once you have the answers to your questions, understand that you are capable of making decisions as well as being

successful. Your focus should be on building self-confidence. You need to take steps to prepare for it. Because thinking can never hurt you or benefit you, but taking action is more important than thinking. If you will do something then the result of your work can be received. Therefore, self-confidence and preparation for self-confidence are very important

for taking decisions.

"The key to success is confidence. The key to self-confidence is preparation "- Arthur Ash"

until you have a clear idea of your goal and destination, till then, you can't hold decision properly. If you are well aware of the consequences of your decision, but think that the obstacles may change the outcome, then make a list of some important facts to get the right result. Divide your work based on this list. Dividing work means doing more than one part of your decision. In this way your attention will be diverted from the difficulties that come along the way. Because dividing decisions and work will also divide difficulties. As the difficulties subsided, our faith increased. We make a hold on the steps. We never learn anything directly. It is also important to learn to cry and laugh before speaking and then a

hoarse voice, so that we can reach the result only by taking one step at a time. Start drawing your steps

with the strength of faith. Better results can be grown than expected. Take your time before making a decision, but never let it weaken after you make a decision. Divert your attention from rumors and

focus your all attention only on the decision. Your decision can prove that you can disprove the rumors. Nature also supports you according to your thinking and courage. There is need to walk alone from home, the caravan is formed automatically. Those who

walk on the paths meet, but those who make the path themselves are rare.

"I don't walk on the roads, when I walk the roads are built, caravans have been witnesses to this truth for centuries." Surjit Pater

Look at your past life, at that time you may find many things impossible. That has become possible today. If one had the desire, the faith, to make the impossible possible, then he would have succeeded. So never let your thinking be helpless, because thinking cannot develop under restrictions. If you want to fly, think first. Build the sky of your dreams.

"I don't believe in making the right decision, I make the decision and make it right" - Ratan Tata

Time changes always. If the darkness of sorrow is

overwhelming over your life, one day there must be the sun of happiness rise that will bring

happiness. All this needs hard work and patience, life changes its color itself. We need to keep our thinking positive and strong so that we can enjoy every color

of life. It is often seen in the society that we can fall to any extent to be happy after suffering from sorrows. We learn to move forward, whether we know how to pull someone back, whether someone praised us or not, we have mastered in the art of criticizing

someone. Evil thinking can never benefit anyone. So we need to take some time to understand life before embarking on the never-ending path of hatred.

When we understand life then we will understand the real happiness of life. Everyone makes their life honorable with their luck and hard work. By thinking badly of someone, we can ruin some of their precious time but we cannot take them away from their destination and dreams. On the contrary, our poor attitude towards him motivates him to work

harder and reach his dreams. Then why are we ready to fall in someone's eyes for our false happiness.

Every word that comes out of our mouths put bad impact on our character and relationship. Because the wounds of the sword will heal in time, but the

wounds of the tongue will never heal up. That is why we need to get out of the false world of pretense and bring simplicity and sweetness in our life.

"Make a list of your own decisions and the decisions made by others. Try to examine the results that you got from these decisions. After comparing learn to develop the skill of decision-making."

CHAPTER FOURTEEN

Start living for yourself

Life becomes too short for those who live and too big for those who cut. Sometimes we get so caught up in responsibilities that we don't even have time for

ourselves. Happiness feels like an autumn tree

without family and friends. Happiness waits your family and friends, just as autumn waits spring to sprout new crumbs. Complications in family problems and spending some time with family are two different things. You must have some time in

your daily life for your family and friends. There are very few friends who stand in sorrows. In times of

happiness even if we are surrounded by crowds. But there will be very few of your true friends in this crowd. Everyone else you talk to will be a part of your life. They may be attached to you in one way or another. So keep few friends but keep as many

special friends as you can. In front of which you do

not have to speak thoughtfully. Let them know your every habit. As long as you fulfill the meaning of

others, you live life for others, there is no one better than you when you start living life for yourself, more than half of the relationships are broken. So never

waste your time on broken relationships.

"You have limited time, don't waste it living for someone else" - Steve Jobs

Relationships are not where everything is done thoughtfully. Fear of breaking up weak relationships destroys our happiness. Living for yourself does not mean living alone, it means living in a different world of your own. Where your special friends and family members can witness your happiness. Sometimes we associate happiness with money. We feel that

happiness is impossible without money. But

happiness is not really about money at all. Money can only meet your needs or give you some materialistic pleasures. The more money will you have, the less time you have for your family. You will make artificial happiness a part of your life. With money big pools can be built, but the feeling of bathing in the rain cannot be felt. So create happiness, a different

world of happiness resides in the bosom of nature.

"Take a closer look at nature and you'll get to know everything better" Albert Einstein

The sound of birds chirping in the morning can fill you with joy. In cold weather, the rays of sun will cut the fog and will realize warm welcome of happiness to you. The redness of the sun, the light of the moon

will want to open its arms and take you in the bosom of happiness. These joys have no value. There is a little difference between pretend happiness and real happiness. Sometimes we cannot understand this difference and get confused in pretend happiness.

Just as the fragrance of artificial flowers cannot be perceived, so the serenity of artificial and pretend pleasures cannot be felt.

Get in touch with laughter so much that the pain

starts to subside. If you keep a positive outlook, you will find that every aspect of life is a source of

happiness, and a negative outlook can make

happiness even more miserable. Happiness has to do with your dreams and hobbies. Living for yourself

means living for your dreams and hobbies. You must give your time to those works that can bring

happiness on your face and give relaxation. Don't let your hobbies be vanished under the pressure of

responsibilities. Hobbies never end alone; they take with them both happiness and tranquility.

"Accept the responsibilities of your life. Know that you can take yourself where you want to go. No one else will take you - Les Brown.

So we need to work on ourselves. Our joys and

sorrows can change our meaning because of our attitude. If we think positive then life will open millions of doors for us, of happiness and victory.

Negative thinking on the other hand will create

millions of obstacles and excuses, which will not only make us sad but also deprive us of happiness. Look positively at the accidents and business activities

happening around you. If you create a happy atmosphere around you in addition to work, you will not feel tired at work. The results from work will be better than before. In addition, if you will work in a happy environment, you will go home with

happiness. This change will start a new beginning for your family. A start that allows you to spend quality time with your family. Our relationships will only get stronger if we will talk in home. Sometimes

responsibilities do not allow you to focus on your family. This neglect has a profound effect on your children and your spouse's heart. They begin to break down in within. These circumstances start to chonk the neck of your happiness. If you don't get your

family out of this grip ahead of time, you will take

your happiness away from yourself. You should try to leave the tensions of job and business there. Your personal time should be focused on the family. This time will bring you closer to your spouse. You will be able to understand your partner's feelings and spend some memorable moments for their unfulfilled desires.

"Make a list of your happiness and your dreams.
Strengthen relationships with those whom with you can
share these joys. Make time for yourself "

CHAPTER FIFTEEN

Victories and defeats are a part of life, not life.

Life goes on its way, victories and defeats keep coming back and forth during this journey. Victory

gives us happiness and defeat sorrow. But we should welcome both victory and defeat with a smile because victory is associated with our hard work and our dreams, so becoming happy is sure. But often we are saddened by defeats but we should think positively, if we lose then what we get in the form of experience, we cannot win every time. The habit of winning creates a feeling of pride in us. We get the

superstition that we can't defeat. As a result, we tend to ignore hard work and the right way. This behavior turns our victory into defeat. Victory or defeat can never fully describe your ability. So whatever the

outcome, you should be happy all the time. If you

will find, there must be some happiness in defeat too.You can't find a person in the whole world who wins every time, if you will search it all your life but still you have to return empty handed. From this we must understand that there is no existence of victories

without defeats, just as there is no happiness without sorrow. Gain experience from your defeats. Try to learn something new constantly, you will soon be able to strengthen your grip on victories and defeats.

"Winning or losing is part of the game, it should not be taken to heart."- Milkha Singh

Sometimes easy ways can save you from suffering. But it is not certain whether they will give happiness or not. Difficult paths will not only bring you

happiness, but also experience will be the cause of

happiness in your life. See big dreams, small dreams can see everyone, even if you fail once or twice, the

journey to small dreams will be completed even if you move towards big defeat. Nothing is ever

achieved without difficulty and effort, even a mother feeds her baby from crying. If even the deepest

shadow of God's form Mother treats the child in this way. So how can you expect from life that it will give you everything in happiness without any difficulty and effort.

"For big wins, take big risks" - Bill Gates

The seeds of your happiness are hidden in every difficulty and sorrow. Only from these seeds the trees of happiness can be grown. If you can absorb the heat of difficulties in your heart. Time and experience will turn this heat of yours into a fire. By controlling this

organ properly, you will be able to eradicate the darkness of sorrows and create the light of happiness. How long this light lasts will determine your thinking and your efforts. Nature's law is that the strong always suppress the weak. It is now up to you to weaken the pain or to weaken yourself.

"If you want to shine like the sun, first learn to burn like it." -APJ Abdul Kalam

Your positive thinking will make you a game changer. Everyone plays the game. If you don't want to live like everyone else, then your hard work and dreams

should be different from people. Come to understand this fact better. Let's try to understand an example.

The eagle is 70 years old but after the age of 30 it

starts to change. Which upsets his life. Three things happen to him.

1. The claws of his claws become too long which makes his grip on the prey weak.
2. His beak turns more than necessary. This makes it difficult for him to eat the prey.

3. His wings become so heavy that it becomes

impossible to catch the prey, his life becomes worse than death, then he has only 3 options left.

1. Give up your body with hunger.
2. Let go of your nature and start eating dead prey like a vulture.
3. The third option is the most frightening, changes in the body but the eagle likes to choose this painful and difficult option. He starts this process by building a nest on the top of a mountain for a difficult and long process of 150 days. First, he breaks his beak by

hitting it with a mountain and there is no more painful than it for him, after sometime when beak comes again, he pull out his nails with own beak, there is nothing worse than it he pull out nails by

oneself. The next step is that he starts to pull out his wings. After plucking the wings one by one with his beak, he just waits till the new wings to come and the nails grow again by the passage of 150 days his beak becomes as strong as before. The claws that make

strength on the prey become even stronger and have new wings with him for his new flight. Now with a better change, he can fly higher than before. It gives us the courage to face adversity. Happiness after sorrow and victory after defeat is inevitable. Make defeat and victory a part of your life, if you give them the right to dominate the whole life then it will be

your own fault. Learn to forget every bad accident. Some accidents may not push you back, but they will try to stop from moving forward. Defeat becomes

your past, thinking of defeat you welcome the

sorrows. If you can't change the past then there is no point of worrying about the past. Take a look at your past and try to find out. What was the real reason for your defeat? This may be due to your lack of effort,

straying from the right direction or being unaware of your challenge. Separating experience from the past leaves only sorrows in the lap of the past. Forget these sorrows, move on.

"No one can go back and start, but they can start today and end a new," said Marie Robinson

Light also changes its meaning over time. The light from which we seek warmth in winter. In the same light we feel heat in summer. So understand that nothing is permanent.

Learn to enjoy the results, no one conversate about difficulties. Your joys and

sorrows will lose their meaning like the light of the sun. So feel them at the right time. Be prepared to

welcome them and dare to say goodbye. If you learn to adapt yourself according to the situation. The courage to change the situation will be born in you automatically. In the face of defeat, you develop such qualities that you will no longer be afraid of the consequences of both victories and defeats. Whenever we stop being afraid of the consequences, peace and happiness begin to find us. Not being afraid of the consequences means that the habit of losing or winning can never overwhelm your

intellect. But this does not mean that ignoring hard work and dedication, in fact becoming not afraid of the consequences is your intelligence. There is very

little difference between carelessness and negligence. Only those who learn the art of understanding these nuances become expert to turn victories into defeats. Sometimes we think that our hard work was the same but the result of the other was good and why my

result was bad. Why doesn't it give us a chance to understand that in our point of view the skill of

understanding the nuances may be less than others. But before we reach the right cause, we are doomed to failure. Keep striving in the right direction, never let your dreams get blurred in the dust of difficulties. One day you will reach your goal. With the help of excuses like helplessness and luck

you cannot move forward but the habit of these

supports will definitely cripple you. You will stop trying to reach happiness. Defeat of any kind is defeat, but fighting the situation, doing competition, is far more honorable than defeating effortless.

Instead of fearing the consequences of losing, focus your attention on those works that associate with victory. Success arises itself from hard work .

To understand the extent to which positive and negative thinking can affect our lives, let us share an example: When a prisoner was sentenced to death in the United States, some scientists thought why not do some experiments on this prisoner. Then the prisoner was told that if you were hanged you would die in agony and if we killed you by stinging you with a poisonous cobra instead of hanging you would die

soon. The prisoner chose the path of stinging from the snake.

After a large venomous snake was brought in front of him, the prisoner was blindfolded and tied to a chair, and pain was given with a safety pen instead of

stinging from stake. The prisoner died in a few

seconds after the safety pin was bitten. An autopsy

revealed that the dead prisoner's body contained the same venom as the snake's venom.

Now where did this poison come from that took the life of the prisoner ... that poison was produced by his body in shock. Our every concept produces positive and negative energy and it produces hormones according to our body. 75% of diseases and the root cause of a sad life generate from the energy that come from negative thinking. Today mankind is

destroying itself because of its wrong thinking.

Always keep your thinking positive and be happy. At the age of 25, a person doesn't care what will people think? Until the age of 50, people live in fear of what people will think? Then, 50 years later, it turns out that no one cares about us. Let's get rid of the fear of what people will think. Man feels what he thinks, whether positive or negative.

Highlight the victories and defeats in your life. Feel the victory, make a list of the experiences gained from the defeats and start acting on it.

CHAPTER SIXTEEN

Learn the art of reading silent faces

Many lives are being nurtured in the bosom of nature. Everyone is given the art of expressing their feelings, gestures. The best art has come in the destiny of a human being. He can share his feelings and emotions by talking. He can also read, write, and listen. All of these become a way for him to feel emotions, sorrow, happiness. The same thing can be done in different ways. How much love there is in

your relationship. It determines the way of your communication. Speak humbly at all times, think before speaking and speak appropriately because the arrow that come out of the bow and the words come out of the tongue never come back. By taunting

someone, talking can ruin a lifelong relationship. It is very easy to understand each other through conversation. But not everything can be shared with everyone. For that, there should be a strong

foundation of love and trust in your relationship. Sometimes life bring a person to such a point that he

cannot speak even he wants to. At this point he needs to feel and understand that silence can only be heard by those who care about each other who know each

other well. Even in a smiling face, a sad person would be hidden. Those who love you will understand by

reading your face. Just like a mother can feel the pain of a child without speaking, listen to your partner's

silence to increase the love in your relationship, read his face. If at the right time you understand

someone's silent feelings and emotions. That way you can save many lives. You can show the way to sad and disoriented people. Because silence becomes a disease within which people either become depressed or think of committing suicide. Even in the world of crime, those people walk whom could not feel anyone or whose Silence could not find a word. All this

happens due to a weak mindset and a weak mindset is also born from the womb of suppressed aspirations. So try to build trust in the relationship so that nothing turns into silence. This art is very much needed in every relationship. Parents in particular

need to be proficient in this art. Because children are very sensitive. They feel the smallest detail. This

surrounding environment leaves a deep impression on their minds. Parents need to maintain a close and loving relationship with their children. With the help of this relationship children will be able to do everything well with their parents. It also gives children a chance to understand the hidden qualities in them. If we want to live in a good and healthy

society then let's break each other's silence, read the fake masked face and meet the real face ', let's clear the dust from our thinking. This step of ours will

work to end crime and fill the sweetness of love in relationships. It is also true that every relationship has a limit. But crime happens where there are more restrictions. By capturing water in the rivers we can give direction it as we wish but the storm created

from these rivers causes catastrophe. There are also storms in the ocean, but there is no destruction in its water as is done by water controlled by dams, because the ocean is so vast without restrictions, he also knew his edges. The existence of freedom in our

country and abroad is different. Foreign countries are also free in thought. But our thinking is enslaved, our society does not provide an environment to

understand and feel each other, which is why rape and many other crimes are increasing day by day, humanity is dying. Let's understand each other, create love, trust in mutual relationships and end silence and crime. Keep your mind free.

- "The greatest discovery of my generation is that man can change his life by changing his attitude - William James

oLet's change the attitude of being alone and start sharing our joys and sorrows. Each character has different feelings and emotions for each accident.

Never make fun of another's feelings. Because of your fear of ridicule, some people make loneliness a part of their lives and silence their habit. Happiness meaning for a child, for a young and for the elderly is something else. The meaning of physical relation for an unmarried girl something else and something else for a married girl. For a widow, the meaning of physical contact is different from both. This difference does not end there.

For everyone this relationship becomes a new feeling. So we should understand everyone. If we are happy in our lives, it does not mean that we

should try to change the lives of people who are living their lives with some incomplete feelings and

sadness, don't try to turn their helplessness into

silence. We need to understand the mindset of a sad partner. To understand someone's pain, one has to stand in his place and think like him. Just as a coin has two sides, so does every accident in life have

more than one side. By the way, happiness can be found only by sharing happiness with others. But some people learn to be happy alone. They find

peace in solitude. But not everyone living alone can be calm. So for understanding loneliness, examine your partner's nature and circumstances. Giving

happiness to others will give you a feeling of blissful peace inside. Learn to share happiness and love

without any meaning.

"Sometimes happiness become a cause of smiling. But sometimes our smile become the cause of our

happiness ... -Tick Naat Haan

Everyone joins in the joy. These joys become even more honorable if you try to get someone out of loneliness by supporting them in their pain. When we get too busy with responsibilities and get away from

family happiness. At that time it takes time to live for oneself. But we cannot say that living for oneself

means living for oneself. Your self includes your

family and your friends. So learn to share happiness with your loved ones. In order to diminish sadness and loneliness in your surrounding environment you would have to be partner of them. For making new relationships, there can't be better way than sharing

happiness. When we begin to understand others then surely others will also begin to understand us. Better a poor horse than no horse at all.

"Make a list of old relationships. Try to find out the reason for their breakdown. Question to every silence in your life.:

The whole game of life depends on your thinking.

Your point of view can make the impossible to possible. This power should be used to feel and share happiness.

"If you don't want to get caught up in the waves, learn the art of sieging the waves."

www.ingramcontent.com/pod-product-compliance
Lightning Source LLC
Chambersburg PA
CBHW052050150726
48002CB00002B/826